Tiptoe Into Scary Cities

WRETCHED WASHINGTON

by Spencer Brinker

Consultant: Debbie Felton
Professor of Classics
University of Massachusetts
Amherst, Massachusetts

BEARPORT PUBLISHING

New York, New York

Credits

Cover, © Dmytrolshchenko/Shutterstock and © trekandshoot/Shutterstock; TOC, © Tono Balaguer/Shutterstock; 4–5, © CE Photography/Shutterstock, © Andrei Medvedev/Shutterstock, and © Library of Congress; 6L, © frankie's/Shutterstock; 6R, © Ian Dagnall Commercial Collection/Alamy; 7, © Hu Totya/GFDL; 8, © Everett-Art/Shutterstock, © avevizavi_com/Shutterstock, and © Combatcamerauk/Shutterstock; 9, © Marshall Ikonography/Alamy and © BlueSkyImage/Shutterstock; 10L, © Alexander Gardner/Library of Congress; 10R, © Library of Congress; 11, © Orhan Cam/Shutterstock; 12L, © Library of Congress; 12R, Public Domain; 13, © Jack E. Boucher/Library of Congress and © Everett Historical/Shutterstock; 14L, © vilax/Shutterstock; 14R, © University of Texas at Austin; 15, © Orhan Cam/Shutterstock; 16 (L to R), © North Wind Picture Archive, © Gilbert Stuart, and © Bess Otis; 17, © National Park Service; 18–19, © Keith Lamond/Shutterstock; 18T, © Universal Images Group North America/Alamy; 18B, © Eric Isselee/Shutterstock and © 4contrast_dot_com/Shutterstock; 20, © Eric Isselee/Shutterstock; 21, © Architect of the Capitol; 23, © Konstantin L/Shutterstock; 24, © Tono Balaguer/Shutterstock.

Publisher: Kenn Goin
Senior Editor: Joyce Tavolacci
Creative Director: Spencer Brinker
Photo Researcher: Thomas Persano
Cover: Kim Jones

Library of Congress Cataloging-in-Publication Data

Names: Brinker, Spencer, author.
Title: Wretched Washington / by Spencer Brinker ; consultant, Debbie Felton, Professor of Classics, University of Massachusetts, Amherst, Massachusetts.
Description: New York : Bearport Publishing Company, Inc., 2019. | Series: Tiptoe into scary cities | Includes bibliographical references and index.
Identifiers: LCCN 2018014149 (print) | LCCN 2018025703 (ebook) | ISBN 9781684027095 (ebook) | ISBN 9781684026630 (library)
Subjects: LCSH: Haunted places—Washington (D.C.)—Juvenile literature. | Ghosts—Washington (D.C.)—Juvenile literature.
Classification: LCC BF1472.U6 (ebook) | LCC BF1472.U6 B7275 2018 (print) | DDC 133.109753—dc23
LC record available at https://lccn.loc.gov/2018014149

For more information, write to Bearport Publishing Company, Inc., 45 West 21st Street, Suite 3B, New York, New York 10010. Printed in the United States of America.

10 9 8 7 6 5 4 3 2 1

Contents

WRETCHED WASHINGTON

A trip to Washington, DC, is like a walk through history. But after feeling cold chills and hearing ghostly voices, you may wonder: *Is some of the history still alive?*

Get ready to read four scary stories about **wretched** Washington. Turn the page . . . if you dare!

Beware of George!

The Old Stone House

One of the oldest buildings in our nation's **capital** is a small stone house. It was built over 250 years ago.

Yet the Old Stone House is more than a piece of the past. It's also said to be home to many **spirits**! One of them is a **savage** ghost named George.

A bedroom in the Old Stone House

The Old Stone House

Visitors have heard the laughter of unseen children inside the Old Stone House. They've spotted ghosts dressed in clothes from long ago. Of all the spirits, George is the most feared.

When George is around, guests have felt cold as ice. And they were seized by **dread**. Then, invisible hands gripped their necks. Is George playing another cruel prank?

The Old Stone House was almost torn down in the 1950s. Some people fought to save it. They believed George Washington had stayed in the house.

Inside the Old
Stone House

Who's There?

The White House

In 1942, Queen Wilhelmina of the Netherlands was staying at the White House. Suddenly, she heard a knock on her door. When she opened it, Abraham Lincoln's ghost stood before her. She was so spooked that she fainted.

Queen Wilhelmina

The White House

Not long before that, workers ran from the White House after seeing Lincoln's ghost. Once, British Prime Minister Winston Churchill was startled by the spirit.

Winston Churchill

In the 1980s, White House **foreman** Tony Savoy saw Lincoln's ghost, too. "When I turned the light on one morning, he was sitting there. . . . And when I blinked, he was gone!"

Willie Lincoln

People have also seen the ghost of Lincoln's son in the White House. Willie Lincoln died there when he was just 11 years old.

The Lincoln Bedroom in the White House

A Sweet-Smelling Ghost

The Octagon House

Visitors to Washington often stop at the Octagon House. In spite of its name, the house has only six sides, not eight. What's an even bigger surprise? Sometimes, the house is filled with the smell of lilac flowers. That's when a ghostly woman appears out of nowhere!

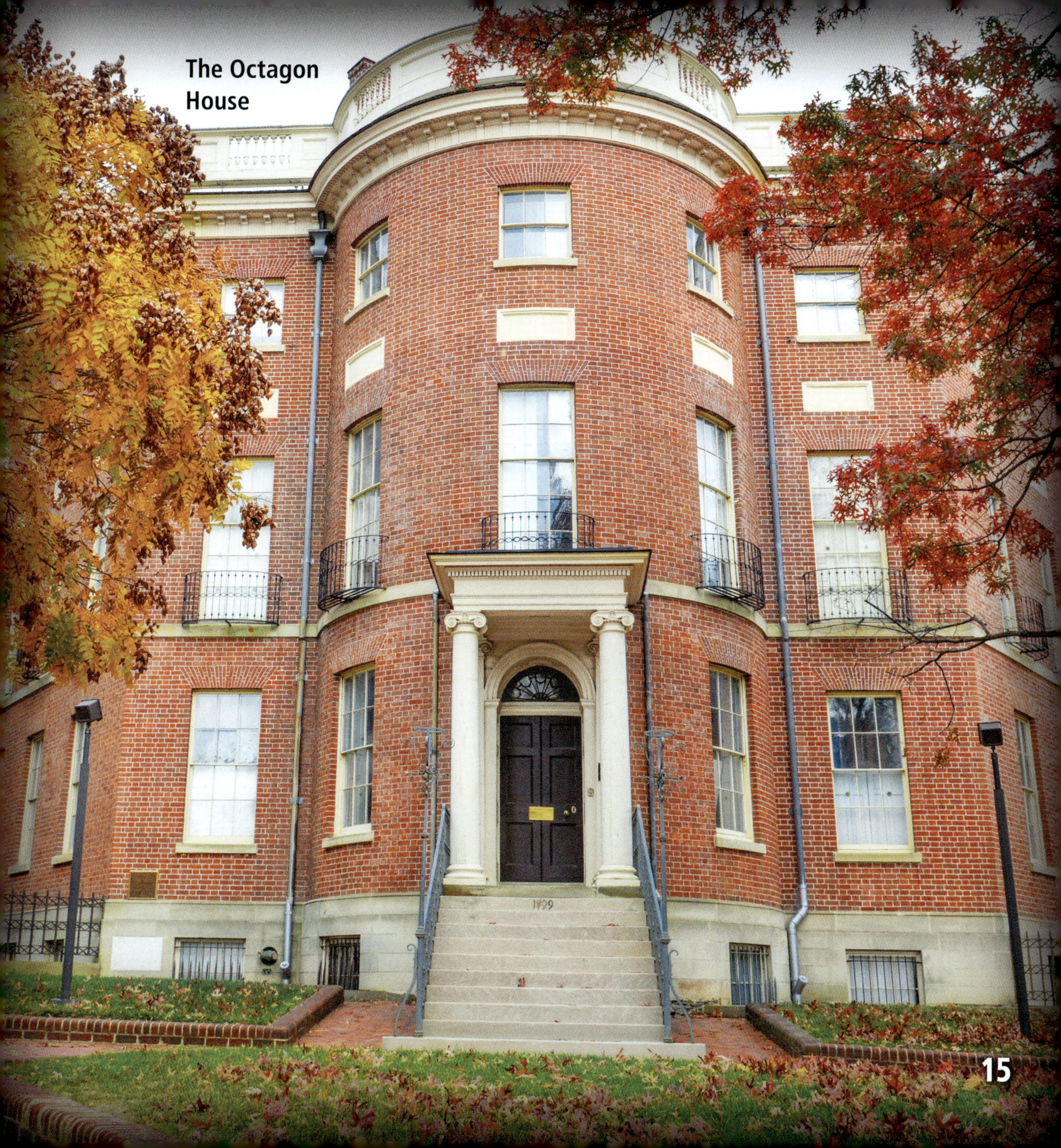

The Octagon House

In 1814, the British set fire to the White House. President James Madison and his wife, Dolley, then moved into the Octagon House. It seems that Dolley, or rather her ghost, has never left.

The White House burning in 1814

President James Madison

First Lady Dolley Madison

Dolley's spirit has been seen floating in the halls of the house. People have also heard the sounds of **phantom** parties. Dolley loved to host gatherings. What was her favorite flower? Take a guess.

Ghostly bells have long been heard ringing in the Octagon House. Who do they belong to?

THE DEMON CAT

The United States Capitol Building

It's said that ghostly soldiers and long-dead presidents haunt the **Capitol** Building. But not all of the ghosts look like people. A black **demon** cat with glowing eyes is known to **prowl** the building.

The United States Capitol Building

Soon after the Capitol Building was built, workers brought cats there to kill rats. One of the cats may still be living there—long after it died.

Night workers have seen a black cat with glowing yellow eyes. When the men walk toward it, the cat grows to the size of a tiger. Then, the demon cat leaps—and disappears midair!

The US Capitol Crypt

The demon cat is said to make its home in a **crypt**. The crypt was built for President George Washington.

Spooky Spots in Washington, DC

The Old Stone House

History has a way of sneaking up on you.

The White House

A long-dead president is waiting to greet you.

The Octagon House

If you smell lilacs, get ready to meet a ghost!

The United States Capitol Building

Watch out for a spooky cat with glowing eyes.

Glossary

capital (KAP-uh-tuhl) a city where a country's government is based

capitol (KAP-uh-tuhl) the building that serves as the center of government

crypt (KRIPT) an underground room where people are often buried

demon (DEE-muhn) an evil spirit

dread (DRED) a strong feeling of fear

foreman (FOR-muhn) a person in charge of a group of workers

phantom (FAN-tuhm) ghostly

prowl (PROUL) to move sneakily around

savage (SAV-ij) dangerous or violent

spirits (SPEER-itz) supernatural creatures, such as ghosts

wretched (RECH-ihd) very bad or unpleasant

Index

Read More

Lunis, Natalie. *A Haunted Capital (Scary Places).* New York: Bearport (2014).

Markovics, Joyce. *Chilling Cemeteries (Tiptoe Into Scary Places).* New York: Bearport (2017).

Learn More Online

To learn more about wretched Washington, visit:
www.bearportpublishing.com/Tiptoe

About the Author

Spencer Brinker lives and works in New York City. He used to live in Washington, DC. While he was there, he says he unfortunately never met any of the city's ghosts.